S0-BED-967

A Tundra Wilderness

by Kitt Winston

Harcourt

SCHOOL PUBLISHERS

Cover, ©age fotostock/SuperStock; p.4, ©Prisma/SuperStock; p.5, ©Tui De Roy/Minden Pictures; p.6, ©Raymond Gehman/National Geographic/Getty Images; p.7, (tc) ©THOMAS MANGELSEN/ Minden Pictures, (l) ©PhotoDisc; p.8, ©JIM BRANDENBURG/Minden Pictures; p.9, ©Eastcott/ Momatiuk/Animals Animals; p.10, ©FLIP NICKLIN/Minden Pictures; p.11, ©WINFRIED WISNIEWSKI/ FOTO NATURA/Minden Pictures; p.12, ©Johnny Johnson/Animals Animals; p.13, ©David E. Myers/ Stone/Getty Images; p.14, ©PhotoDisc/PunchStock.

Cartography, p.3, Joe LeMonnier

Printed in Hong Kong

ISBN 10: 0-15-350985-6
ISBN 13: 978-0-15-350985-8

Ordering Options
ISBN 10: 0-15-350601-6 (Grade 4 On-Level Collection)
ISBN 13: 978-0-15-350601-7 (Grade 4 On-Level Collection)
ISBN 10: 0-15-357938-8 (package of 5)
ISBN 13: 978-0-15-357938-7 (package of 5)

4 5 6 7 8 9 10 0940 12 11 10 09

It is the end of the winter on the tundra. For months, days have had few, if any, hours of sunlight. As daylight grows longer, the tundra awakens with life. The top layer of ice begins to melt. The soil becomes warmer. First come plants, then insects. As spring arrives, animals return to this frozen land. Although, some animals stay on the tundra year-round.

The tundra is an area of remarkable land at the top of the Earth near the North Pole. Because this part of the Earth tilts away from the sun during winter, the tundra receives little light and energy from the sun. The plants and animals that live in the tundra have adapted to live and survive in the cold.

Shaded areas show the tundra

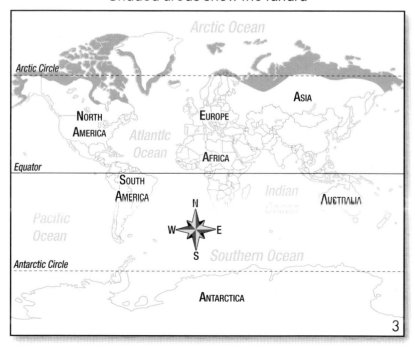

The top layer of soil in the tundra is frozen during most of the year. Below that, there is a layer of ice that is there year-round. To observe the tundra in winter, you would think it is a place that has no life. The land is covered with rocks and snow, and there are no trees. However, if you look closely, you will find a world of plants and animals that comes to life each spring.

During the winter, many plants are dormant, or not active, beneath the frozen soil. When the top layer of soil warms and begins to thaw in the spring, these plants come alive. As the soil thaws, plants bud and begin to grow.

Mosses and cushion plants are suitable for the tundra climate. They grow low to the ground and close together. This protects them from the wind. Air pockets form between layers of leaves and on moss, trapping the heat. The season for growing in the tundra is extremely short. It is less than two months.

In the spring, many insect eggs hatch in the tundra. Soon there are bees, flies, and butterflies flitting about.

During the winter, flocks of birds fly south. They go to warmer places where food can be easily found. When the heat of the sun warms the tundra, many birds return to make their nests and lay eggs. Plants and insects in the tundra make up much of the food that birds eat.

Great waves of birds can be seen over the tundra skies in the springtime. Some birds, like the tundra swan, migrate, or travel, very long distances in the winter. These birds can fly as far away as Europe, Canada, or the United States. In spring and summer, the tundra swans return. They make their homes in the lakes and ponds that dot the area.

Ptarmigan

Snowy owl

Another tundra bird is the snowy owl. The owl feeds on small animals, such as hares or squirrels. Snowy owls make their nests in hollows in the ground. They line the nests with mosses and feathers.

Some birds are adapted to live in the tundra all year long. The ptarmigan [tär-mi-gên] changes colors with the seasons. In the winter, the bird's feathers are white. This helps it to stay hidden in the icy, winter landscape. In spring, however, the bird's feathers turn brown. The bird now matches the brown colors of springtime. Blending into the landscape helps protect the birds from animals that would hunt them for food.

Many tundra animals have fur that changes color with the seasons. The arctic hare has fur that is gray-brown in the summer. In the winter, its fur turns white. The changing color of the fur helps the hare hide from stealthy animals such as foxes that would hunt it for food.

Arctic hares build nests for their young in the spring. The female hare will dig a small hole in the ground behind a rock or a bush. Then she lines the nest with grass and fur. The hares feed on plant twigs, roots, and sometimes berries.

Arctic foxes also have fur that changes color with the seasons. In summer, its fur is a pretty blue-gray color. In the winter, its fur changes into a creamy white so that it can blend in with the snow.

Arctic foxes eat squirrels, birds' eggs, or the leftover kill of polar bears. The arctic foxes need to be careful, though. Foxes are a favorite food of the polar bear!

Arctic fox

Like many tundra animals, polar bears spend the summer eating food to fatten up for the long winter ahead. Unfortunately for seals, they are the polar bears' favorite food. Polar bears spend most of the summer in search of seals. In fact, polar bears can swim to find seals. These bears are often found looking for seals on sheets of floating ice many miles from land. The polar bear also eats fish. It extracts them from the water with its large, powerful paws.

As the days of spring pass into summer, the hours of sunlight grow longer. During summer in the tundra, the sun never really sets. It may dip out of sight for a few minutes. Then it appears in the summer sky again. It is daylight for nearly twenty-four hours.

In early summer, birds like the swan and snowy owl hatch from their eggs. Foxes and wolves may hunt for young birds that cannot yet fly. As summer passes, the young birds lose their down feathers and grow feathers for flight.

Snowy owl nest

In summer, arctic hares are born in their furry nests. Arctic foxes give birth in the summer, too. The male fox guards the den and brings food to the mother.

Soon the days of summer come to an end. Each day, there is less sunlight. The temperatures begin to drop. The animals now must prepare for the long, cold winter ahead. Young tundra swans are only about three months old when they must make the journey south. Snowy owls make the winter journey to Canada. There, they take advantage of the plentiful food.

Baby arctic foxes

Arctic ground squirrel

In winter, arctic foxes build their dens in the sides of snowbanks. The foxes have thick fur on their paws that help them walk over the frozen land. They also dig holes deep into the frozen ground where they hide food. The cold ground keeps the food fresh for the foxes to eat.

Some animals hibernate during the winter. Hibernation is a sleep-like state during which the animal uses very little energy. Polar bears and ground squirrels prepare for the winter by digging dens. The squirrels line their dens with grasses and hair. There, they store food such as leaves and seeds. The bears dig their dens in snowbanks.

As winter falls upon the tundra, the land becomes cold and dark. Flocks of birds have gone south. Insects have laid their eggs to be hatched the next spring. The polar bears and ground squirrels are snug in their dens. Only a few animals remain in the frozen land. The arctic fox, the snowy owl, and the musk ox move about the tundra in search of food. These animals are adapted to withstand the cold winter.

As the winter months pass, and spring arrives, the tundra awakens once again. Soon the sun shines over the land. The cycle of plant and animal life starts all over again.

Think Critically

1. What are some tundra animals that travel in search of food?

2. How do fur and feathers that change colors with the seasons help animals survive in the tundra?

3. What do polar bears do after the summer is over?

4. Why do you think polar bears are often found floating on sheets of ice in the summer?

5. Would you like to visit the tundra? Tell why or why not.

Science

The Changing Tundra Many animals in the tundra change colors to protect themselves. Look in a reference book or on the Internet, and find out about other animals that change with the seasons.

 School-Home Connection How do the plants and animals in your neighborhood change as the seasons change? Write a paragraph to explain your ideas.